My Name is Al and I'm the owner of Team Randori Martial Arts, a Martial Arts Academy that specializes in teaching Brazilian Jiu Jitsu (BJJ) and Mixed Martial Arts (MMA). We have two academies. One is located in Annapolis Maryland and the other is in the Silver Spring, Wheaton Maryland area. Throughout my life I've always been fascinated by the Martial Arts. I think if you grew up during the 70's there is no doubt that either Bruce Lee or Chuck Norris were your childhood heroes. And as such we all wanted to be like our heroes. We studied, Wing Chung Kung Fu, Karate, and Tae Kwon Do to mention a few of the arts. Personally, I favored Tae Kwon Do, and actually studied in Seoul Korea, while in the military. I even though I was good at it, as I had earned a Black Belt. Like I said we all wanted to be like our heroes.

As my martial arts career progressed, I studied several martial arts off and on, always coming back to Tae Kwon Do until I met "Pat." Pat was a brown belt in BJJ. He often spoke to me about the efficiency of BJJ and claimed its superiority and effectiveness over other martial arts. I seriously doubted this, and though him a little crazy as during our discussions he could not mention one person that I could relate to from my childhood who could be considered a martial arts hero. BJJ really, who studied BJJ? This was my attitude with Pat for about 6 months, until he finally talked me into training with him. I guess I had had enough and it finally came to the point where I would have to show Pat how wrong he was.

The day we got together, I remember asking Pat if he wanted to wear my head-gear as that I did not want to cause him harm from striking or kicking him in the head. He just looked at me with this crazy look on his face as he downed his incredibly heavy Gi. I thought to myself, "I'm Going to Kill This Guy." We started out slow, I shoot up a couple of kicks, a jab and a couple more kicks. From what I can recall, somehow Pat took me down to the ground, got on top of me and used his heavy Gi to choke me to the point that I almost passed out. I thought to myself, what the "HELL." Pat let me up from off the ground, I recovered and we started again. After a couple of strike and kick attempts, I was back on the ground, this time Pat was hyperextending my arm.

I quickly came to know this technique as an "Arm Bar." This sequence of events went on and on that afternoon. I got my BUTT kicked by a BJJ brown belt. I thought to myself, "Thank God" Pat was not a Black Belt, I probably would not be here writing this today.

After our sparing session, the first words that came out of my mouth, to Pat was "Where Could I Learn BJJ." You see, I pride myself on being a well-educated person and would even go out on a limb and say that I was smart. I quickly come to realize that I had invested a significant period of time and money studying martial arts that in Pat's words were ineffective. The very next day, I enrolled in a BJJ academy, hung up my Tae Kwon Do Gi, and began practicing BJJ.

As I embarked on my BJJ journey, I began to slowly learn the techniques, but often felt overwhelmed. I could not understand when and how to use the techniques while in a live sparring session (Rolling). You see BJJ is not like other martial arts that train in a static setting. In BJJ in order to perfume a technique it has to be done in a dynamic setting. This setting is called "Rolling." And in rolling your opponent is NOT just going to sit there and be a willing participant. You have to try to employ your techniques against your opponent, all the while they are trying to impose their techniques on you. Man is this a GREAT sport???

After a couple of years, of floundering around, trying to improve my BJJ skills and formulate the mythical "Game Plan" that all of my training partners spoke of. I began to do research and think about how could a "Game Plan" be mapped out. How could I annotate and document the techniques that I had learned, chain them together and make a map of sorts that would represent an attack that I was going to use on my opponent.

As you begin to take classes and learn BJJ there are several things that you're going to quickly realize. The most glaring question out of them all is "How Am I Going to Learn and Remember All This Stuff." I know, you feel like your drinking from a fire hose. You're a smart person, right? You have the ability to relatively learn almost anything quickly, right? While in class, you hear comments from the instructor or other students while your rolling like "work your game" or "you'll develop a game, just trust me." As they make these comments you ask yourself "What are they talking about" or "How am I supposed to do that?" Work my game. I have no clue what that is. You also may feel like your "TOTALLY" not grasping this sport. How have the other students done it? How have they learned BJJ and how have they become proficient. You ask yourself, am I going to have to get my "Butt" kicked for the next 5 years before something magically clicks. Trust me we all go through this, and if your anything like me I need to analyze and conceptualize the things I do and most importantly need to know the "WHY"

behind what I'm doing. Before I'm actually able to perform it. This was the reason that I created this workbook.

The Brazilian Jiu Jitsu "Game Plan"

The purpose of this workbook is to be a tool where you can record and document individual techniques, that can be linked to one another to develop a "Game Plan." In actuality, the "Game Plan" is your fighting "Strategy" or "Style."

As you learn different techniques and try to employ them during "live rolling sessions," you'll notice that some of the techniques will work and some will not. You will also begin to notice and begin to pick up on the physical reactions of your opponents and training partners after you have employed a technique and succeeded or failed. These reactions have SIGNIFICANT value not matter if you pulled off the technique or not. They offer you insight as to how someone will react to a particular body movement (reaction) and in turn this affords you the opportunity to plan a subsequent movement (technique) that you can either use to amount an attack, defend or counter an attack. Why would we do this?

The linking or connecting a series of techniques to one another in this workbook is equated to a "Playbook" that is commonly used in other sports to win games or overcome opponents. In essence, your building your "Style" or what equates to in other sports as a "Game Plan."

Here is the problem. When we begin this sport, we try to learn Every technique under the sun. We do this without consideration of developing our own BJJ "Style" or "Game Plan." We feverishly learn from friends, You-tube, training videos, and coaches. The failure in this logic is that without having the understanding of how techniques need to be linked to one another, we fall into the "Jack of All Trades, Master of None" category and our game consists of a "Single Shot Strategy." Yep its accurate to say that you may know a ton of techniques, but the problem is that you have no strategy as how to formulate a logical attack or defense.

"It's Chess not Checkers"

Building Your Game Plan

Section 1 - Documentation of Techniques:

This section of the workbook is for you to describe and document techniques that you learn during classes, seminars or from other means. Here is where all the documentation of the movements and details are noted for future reference. Below is an excerpt of what that section looks like:

NAME OF TECHNIQUE:
DESCRIPTION:

Section 2 - Favorites List:

This section of the workbook is for you to make a list of techniques that your readily familiar with; have understanding of, can perform and feel like your somewhat good at. We will start from the standing position and work through the basic BJJ positions (Mount, Side Mount, Back, Etc...) Below is an excerpt of what that section looks like:

STANDING POSITION:

> ➢ **You will note a standing technique here**

> ➢ **You will note another standing technique here**

> ➢ **And another here**

Section 3 - Designing Your Symbol & Abbreviation Key:

This section of the workbook is for you to make a list of symbols and or abbreviations that you can use to represent your techniques, transitions and reactions of your opponent. Below you can see that we use circles, arrowed lines and triangles to represent your symbols.

 = Type of Position of Technique your performing

 = Transition between Positions

 = Reaction or Defense presented by opponent

Section 4 – Building the Game Plan:

This section of the workbook is where your will begin to formulate a plan. We will **Start with Standing.** – Starting from the standing position, you will place a circle in the middle of your sheet labeling the circle with either the term "Standing" or using an abbreviation for it. Remember all altercations or matches start from standing so this is an appropriate place to start. Keep in mind that you should develop a standing "Game Plan" REGARDLESS if you are good at takedowns or not.

Build from Standing – Next from the "Favorites List" under the "Standing" category choose a technique that your confident in and note it in the circle. For example: You might like to "pull" or "jump closed guard" from the standing position. You will then draw a line to another circle and label this circle "Guard." From there you will start to map a transition from "Closed Guard" to other position (Sweeps, Attacks, Etc..).

Build from Other Positions – Now that you "Have Closed Guard" choose a technique that your familiar with from **Section 2** under the "Closed Guard" portion, draw a line between the circles that represent the techniques (this indicates the transition) and label the circle with the technique you have chosen.

THE PURPOSE OF DOING THIS IS TO HELP YOU THINK ABOUT HOW YOUR GOING TO TRANSITION FROM POSITION TO POSITION, DEAL WITH THE DEFENSESES YOUR OPPONENT MAY PRESENT.

Below is a small example of a Game Plan that would be made from the above dissertation of events:

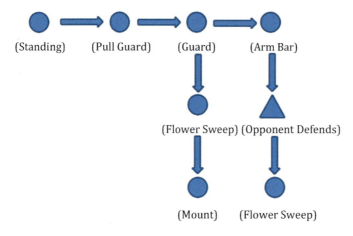

Only add techniques that you like to do, things you are getting good at, or things that you feel may have the potential to fit in your Game Plan. The purpose for doing it this way is that it prevents you from building a "Game Plan" that you're not confident. We are building a "Winning" strategy here!! If your choosing a technique from one of the subcategories in **Section 2** and you realize that you only have one or two that your confident in. Then that's an indicator that you need to learn more techniques and add them to that sub-category. **DON'T JUST ADD SOMETHING TO FILL THE SPACE.**

You Can Make a Separate Game Plan Each Style of BJJ you Train In (Gi or No Gi) If you train No-Gi BJJ make Game Plan for that style. If you train Gi BJJ make Game Plan for that style as well. Due to the similarities between both

styles your Game Plan may be similar in some aspects. However, there are usually ways that some technique or detail may differ per style.

Make Sure You Keep It Simple – This cannot be stressed enough. BJJ is hard enough. Please don't make it harder than what it needs to be!!! Just like with your learning and training your Game Plan should not be super complex. Make them simple and easy to understand. This is your tool, so there is no need to have it look like a plan to build the space shuttle. Keep in mind the easier the plan the less room for error, and in turn your BJJ will be better. Roger Gracie consistently wins with the same simple plan, and everyone knows what that is. Mount and Cross-choke. That's it. Simple.

Begin to Link the Game Plans to One Another – Link Game Plans, portions of them or the whole plan to other plans. This is how you expand your BJJ game. Try to employ the IFTTT principle (If This Than That)

Practice the Game Plan! – This should go without saying. Don't just do all of this research, and formulation and not use it. From our research, this is the number one thing that happens with new students. No dedication to the plan. You need to get a partner, and flow through these Game Plan. Drill the situations over and over again. Break your Game Plans in individual sections of needed and Drill them to get a better understanding and ability to perform them. As you get used to each section it will all come together.

Systemize the Game Plan – The goal is to create a fighting system for yourself, that works, over and over again. Once your confident and can perform the techniques at will it's time to incorporate another technique in the Game Plan.

Review, Revise and Repeat – Always Revisit your Game Plans. While you're not going to completely change your game there are always adjustments or additions to be made. The great BJJ players are great because they have options, movements and techniques that they have incorporated into their game since they were beginners. They have not learned these movements or

techniques and forgot about them, they incorporate them into their Game Plans to establish their style and have over time become very successful at them because they never stopped doing them. They just have the advantage of time over you. They have created Game Plans that they have mastered around techniques they have learned and have built very precise Game Plans around these techniques.

SECTION 1 – TECHNIQUES
(Below annotate a technique and provide a detailed description how to perform it)

NAME OF TECHNIQUE:
DESCRIPTION:

NAME OF TECHNIQUE:
DESCRIPTION:

NAME OF TECHNIQUE:
DESCRIPTION:

SECTION 1 – TECHNIQUES
(Below annotate a technique and provide a detailed description how to perform it)

NAME OF TECHNIQUE:
DESCRIPTION:

NAME OF TECHNIQUE:
DESCRIPTION:

NAME OF TECHNIQUE:
DESCRIPTION:

SECTION 1 – TECHNIQUES

(Below annotate a technique and provide a detailed description how to perform it)

NAME OF TECHNIQUE:
DESCRIPTION:

NAME OF TECHNIQUE:
DESCRIPTION:

NAME OF TECHNIQUE:
DESCRIPTION:

SECTION 2 – MY FAVORITE TECHNIQUES
(Below list three of your favorite techniques under each category)

- **Standing**
    - ➢
    - ➢
    - ➢

- **Mount**
    - ➢
    - ➢
    - ➢

- **Closed Guard**
    - ➢
    - ➢
    - ➢

- **Side Mount**
    - ➢
    - ➢
    - ➢

(Below list three of your favorite techniques under each category)

- **Back Mount**
  - ➢
  - ➢
  - ➢

- **Half Guard**
  - ➢
  - ➢
  - ➢

- **Other Techniques (Etc..)**
  - ➢
  - ➢
  - ➢

SECTION 3 – FAVORITE SUBMISSIONS
(Below list three of your favorite techniques under each category)

- **Submission from Standing**
  - ➢
  - ➢
  - ➢

- **Submission from Mount**
  - ➢
  - ➢
  - ➢

- **Submission from Closed Guard**
  - ➢
  - ➢
  - ➢

- **Submission from Side Mount**
  - ➢
  - ➢
  - ➢

(Below list three of your favorite techniques under each category)

- **Submission from Back Mount**
    - ➢
    - ➢
    - ➢

- **Submission from Half Guard**
    - ➢
    - ➢
    - ➢

- **Other Submissions (Etc..)**
    - ➢
    - ➢
    - ➢

Section 4 - Designing A Game Plan
(Below is an example of a "Game Plan" mapped out)

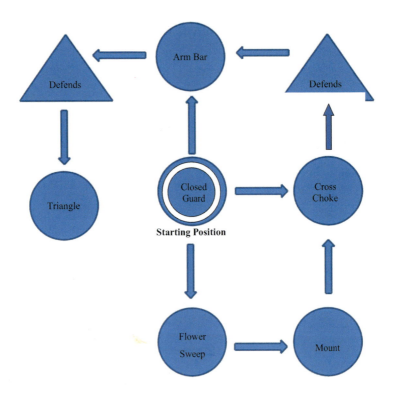

(Use this area to map out a Game Plan)

(Use this area to map out a Game Plan)

(Use this area to map out a Game Plan)

(Use this area to map out a Game Plan)

Okay now that you've learned how to build a couple of "Game Plans." It's time to start implementing them. I ask the student in our Academy to bring their "Game Plan" to class with them. The goal is for them to use what they have mapped out during their live rolls. We ask the student to start with the first position that they noted in their "Game Plan." Their only objective during the roll is to get to this position. It does not matter the length of the roll. Getting into their beginning position establishing the position and control of their opponent is the goal. We are shooting for small success at this point. One inch at a time. Once the student has mastery of getting into this first position their goal is now to transition and get to the next position as reflected in the "Game Plan." This is where it may get tough. Yes, you guessed it the opponent is also trying to implement their game plan at the same time, and they are resistant to the students' movements, and attempts to transition.

Please keep in mind as instructors we DO NOT pair beginners with other beginner students at the same level or who have no experience. We pair the beginner with a slightly more experienced student. One who has made some progression in the development of their game. The paring by instructors is super important. By paring our students this way, the experienced student gets the opportunity to practice their "Game Plan." This advanced student will normally employ 3 – 5 techniques making solid transitions between the techniques. All the while practicing with a student who is resisting them. The student with no experience, and who is just learning their "Game Plan" may not on occasion be able to get into their beginning position, that's ok. As long as an attempt is made, and they note the actions they took, the actions that their opponent took to prevent their implementation, and execution of the technique. All this information and feedback is of super value. All of these actions must be accurately noted, so the student can reflect and make adjustment and corrections.

With the experienced student, the process of having them transition thru a series of techniques actually forces them to perform the techniques over and over, thus enhances their technical ability and mastery of the techniques. The overall goal is to have the student gain the ability to go through one entire chain of linked techniques. Their goal is to employ the techniques, respond to their opponent's reactions, employ the next technique and eventually get to submission. Once the student has the ability to employ a "Game Plan" it's time to start to develop another or to continue refining their initial" Game Plan" but with more experienced BJJ players. I find that at this

point every student is different. Some continue with their initial "Game Plan" and begin to enhance it with other more complex techniques and others simply start over from scratch and build a new "Game Plan." Nevertheless, there is no real correct way to proceed. This is the beauty of BJJ. You get to make your own picture.

The next phase of study is documentation of the roll. Along with the "Game Plan" worksheets, the student uses a note sheet to document their rolls or what they can remember from them. Below is a simple example of a note sheet.

Date of Roll:	Your Rank:
Name of Opponent:	Rank of Opponent:
Technique Used:	

What Worked & Why	What Did not Work & Why

I hope that thru this workbook I was able to help make your introduction to Brazilian Jiu Jitu a little easier and that you actually got something out of it.

Starting Brazilian Jiu Jitsu can be very difficult. I've noticed that normally the phases for students who begin are similar to a bell curve. They begin to go up and are all excited about starting and learning; they then get to a point where they level off and begin to get frustrated due to the inability to perform and conceptualize the information; they then crash back down to their initial phase wherein something happens (a technique clicks, they win a tournament, get promoted, something) and they are then back to phase one where BJJ is intriguing, and exciting and want to learn as much as possible.

As students consume information they then begin to feel as though they're drinking from a firehose in an attempt to gain information. Without knowing it the new student actually begins to suffer from information overload. They want to be good and master all the techniques they have learned. As instructors, we have as much to blame for this "information overload" as the student. Every time they come to class they're taught a new technique.

The Frustration Phase is the phase that with a solid "Game Plan" we are trying to combat or at least shorten. The Frustration Phase occurs after the student has been training for a while. They begin to become frustrated and they feel although they have learned some techniques, nothing that they learned is working. Or they may feel as though they know some techniques, but they really don't know when to employ them. I've often heard students make comment during the frustration phase that they don't know how to document a technique, know when to use it or why they're learning it. It's evident that these students are coming to class, getting technique, after technique, after technique hoping that something will click and that they will wake up one morning knowing Brazilian Jiu Jitsu. During this phase is where this workbook is so valuable.

It's very rare to find someone and this includes their instructors, who explains to them that they need to be able to take the techniques that they have learn and link them together to be successful at Brazilian Jiu Jitsu. I guess it something that is implied. If you have any time on the mat you come to realize this, but with a new student I believe it has to be explained up front. This linkage of techniques enables them to formulate an attack or a defense and to have an understanding of what needs

to be done to be successful at this art. Having a bunch of individual techniques without the ability to link them doesn't enable the student to be successful. Now on occasion you'll find a student who has natural athleticism, or possess a given talent to accidentally link a couple of techniques together. These students are not usually the norm, and their success rate after a while will usually starts to diminish and they two will suffer like their cohorts because they don't incorporate any new techniques in their "Game Plan."

That's why this workbook is so valuable. It gives the student the ability to identify the techniques that they like, the ones they have learned and are able to perform and began to logically, link them together into an order and document that order for future reference and as a guide. I find that at our Academy the students that actually utilize this method of learning are far more successful and advance quicker than the students that don't. It also it shortens the frustration phase, or the "I can't get any technique to work" period dramatically. I truly believe the utilization of this workbook and the learning method can take a student of Brazilian Jiu Jitsu thru their white belt ranks to the black belt ranks all the while providing them with a logical "Game Plan" to employ techniques in concession for almost every situation if they take the time to invest in building a "Game Plan."

So thanks for taking the time to read this little book and I hope it helps you on your Brazilian Jiu Jitsu journey. Good Luck and hope to see you on the mat! Osssss

Made in the USA
Middletown, DE
26 August 2018